Teacher's Resource Book

6

Scott Foresman

Accelerating English Language Learning

Authors

Anna Uhl Chamot

Jim Cummins

Carolyn Kessler

J. Michael O'Malley

Lily Wong Fillmore

Consultant

George González

Longman

Contents

Oral Language Scoring Rubric

To assess a student's progress, complete a copy of the scale on page 3 at the end of each unit.

	Speaking	Fluency	Structure	Vocabulary	Listening
1	Begins to name concrete objects.	Repeats words and phrases.		Uses isolated words.	Understands little or no English.
2	Expresses personal and survival needs; begins to communicate appropriately in discussions and conversations; begins to recall and retell after listening; asks and responds to simple questions.	Expresses ideas in short phrases; speaks hesitantly because of rephrasing and searching for words.	Uses many sentence fragments; has little control over tenses or other grammatical features.	Uses limited, functional vocabulary.	Understands words and phrases; listens attentively for brief periods; requires much repetition; can follow simple (1 or 2 step) oral directions.
3	Initiates and sustains conversation with descriptors and details; exhibits self confidence in social situations; begins to communicate in classroom situations; recalls, retells, and begins to question after listening.	Speaks with occasional hesitation; begins to develop audience awareness; begins to speak with clarity.	Expresses ideas in complete sentences; applies rules of grammar but lacks control of irregular forms (e.g., "writed," "feets," "not never," "more better").	Uses adequate vocabulary but with some irregular word usage.	Understands classroom discussions with repetition, rephrasing, and clarification; begins to maintain attention during a variety of activities; can follow 2–4 step oral directions.
4	Consistently contributes to classroom discussions and conversations; expresses and supports ideas; errors do not interfere with meaning.	Speaks with near native fluency. Any hesitations do not interfere with communication; demonstrates audience awareness and speaks with clarity and confidence.	Uses a variety of structures with occasional grammatical errors.	Uses varied vocabulary.	Understands most spoken language including classroom discussions; follows complex oral directions.

Oral Language Scoring Scale

Name _____

Date _____

Speaking	1	2	3	4
Fluency	1	2	3	4
Structure	1	2	3	4
Vocabulary	1	2	3	4
Listening	1	2	3	4

Reading Skills/Strategies Checklist

Name _____

Date _____

Skill/Strategy	1st 6 weeks	2nd 6 weeks	3rd 6 weeks	4th 6 weeks	5th 6 weeks	6th 6 weeks
Emergent Reader						
Tracks left/right, up/down.						
Uses pictures to retell storyline.						
Uses predictable patterns to tell/recall story.						
Can locate words in a text.						
Can recognize a few words.						
Developing Reader						
Reads short, predictable texts.						
Begins using reading strategies.						
Begins to self-correct.						
Has small, stable sight vocabulary.						
Displays awareness of sounds/symbols.						
Reader						
Reads familiar material on own.						
Uses several reading strategies.						
Figures out words and self-corrects.						
Has large stable sight vocabulary.						
Understands conventions of writing.						
Independent Reader						
Reads appropriate material independently.						
Uses multiple strategies flexibly.						
Makes inferences; draws conclusions.						
Monitors and self-corrects for meaning.						
Chooses to read.						

Comments

Process Writing Checklist

Name _____ Date _____

Writing Process	1st 6 weeks	2nd 6 weeks	3rd 6 weeks	4th 6 weeks	5th 6 weeks	6th 6 weeks
1. Prewriting Strategies						
Chooses topic before writing.						
Decides purpose for writing.						
Outlines or makes graphic organizer.						
Locates details about topic.						
2. Writing Strategies						
Organizes work and workplace.						
Sets goal for writing.						
Refers to notes and graphic organizer.						
Adapts techniques as necessary (e.g., writes without stopping to correct mistakes).						
3. Postwriting Strategies						
Rereads and reviews.						
Gets feedback from others.						
Rewrites and revises.						
Edits and proofreads.						
4. Applications and Interests						
Communicates in writing (letters, etc.).						
Seeks guidance in writing.						
Writes in all curriculum areas.						
Discusses his/her writing.						
Shares writing with others.						
Edits writing of others.						

Comments

Written Language Scoring Rubric

To assess a student's progress, complete a copy of the scale on page 7 at the end of each unit.

	Composing	Style	Sentence Formation	Usage	Mechanics
1	No clear central idea or ideas are apparent to an observer; may be able to read or explain own writing.	Uses known vocabulary in very simple sentences.	Uses frequent non-standard word order; writing contains many run on sentences and sentence fragments.	Shifts from one tense to another; errors in basic conventions.	Rereads to check meaning only; misspells even simple words; makes basic errors in punctuation and capitalization.
2	Shows evidence of central ideas but they are not well focused; can read own writing back to an audience.	Uses basic vocabulary that is not purposefully selected; uses mostly simple declarative sentences.	Uses some non-standard word order; writing contains some run on sentences and sentence fragments.	Makes some errors with inflections, agreement, and word meaning.	Begins to make corrections while writing; makes errors in spelling and punctuation that detract from meaning.
3	Focuses on central ideas but they are not evenly elaborated; includes digressions; utilizes some kind of organization plan.	Uses more varied vocabulary and structures; writes in a variety of forms; beginning to develop a sense of authorship.	Uses mostly standard word order; writing contains some run on sentences or sentence fragments.	Uses mostly standard inflections, agreement, and word meaning.	Recognizes the need to revise and edit and uses revision strategies and the editing process; makes some errors in mechanics that do not detract from meaning.
4	Develops central ideas clearly within an organized and elaborated text; shows confidence as a writer by taking risks.	Purposefully chooses vocabulary and sentence variety; employs a distinctive voice to affect reader; initiates independent writing.	Uses standard word order with no run on sentences or sentence fragments; uses standard modifiers and coordinators and effective transitions.	Uses standard inflections, subject/verb agreement, and standard word meaning.	Uses such conventions as capitalization, punctuation, spelling, and formatting effectively.

Written Language Scoring Scale

Name _____

Date _____

Composing	1	2	3	4
Style	1	2	3	4
Sentence Formation	1	2	3	4
Usage	1	2	3	4
Mechanics	1	2	3	4

Self-Assessment of Oral Language

Name _____

Date _____

Read each statement. Check (✔) the box that is most true for you.

When I use English...	Always	Often	Some-times	Never
Listening				
I can understand many words I hear.				
I can understand the teacher's directions.				
I can understand others when we work in a group.				
I can understand friends outside of class.				
I can understand when the teacher explains something.				
Speaking				
I can name pictures and objects.				
I can ask questions in class.				
I can talk to friends outside of class.				
I can retell a story.				
I can make a presentation in class.				

Self-Assessment of Reading Activities

Name _____

Date _____

Read each statement. Check (✔) the box that is most true for you.

Statement	At Least Once Each Week	At Least Once Each Month	Never or Hardly Ever
I tell a friend about a good book.			
I read about something because I am interested.			
I read on my own outside of school.			
I write about books I have read.			

Statement	Very True of Me	Kind of True of Me	Not at All True of Me
Being able to read is important to me.			
I can understand what I read in school.			
I learn important things from school.			
I am a good reader.			

Other comments about your reading:

_____

_____

_____

Self-Assessment of Writing Activities

Name _____

Date _____

Read each statement. Check (✔) the box that is most true for you.

Statement	At Least Once Each Week	At Least Once Each Month	Never or Hardly Ever
I write letters at home to friends or relatives.			
I take notes when the teacher talks at school.			
I take notes when I read.			
I write a personal response to reading.			
I write a summary of what I read.			
I write stories or poems.			

Statement	Very True of Me	Kind of True of Me	Not at All True of Me
Being able to write is important to me.			
Writing helps me think more clearly.			
Writing helps me tell others what I have learned.			
I am a good writer.			

Other comments about your writing:

_____

_____

My Reading Log

Date	What is the title?	Who is the author?	What did you think of it?

My Writing Log

Date	Working Title	I especially liked:	My readers liked:	What's next?

Anecdotal Record of Reading Skills and Strategies

Name _____

Date _____

Reading Selection

Title _____ Pages _____

Type (circle as many as apply)

    fiction   nonfiction   poetry

    biography   content text   other:

Context (circle one)

    individual   small group   large group

Fluency in reading aloud (pauses, miscues, etc.)

Comprehension (recalls main ideas and details)

Strategies (e.g.: uses prior knowledge, predicts, infers meaning, etc.)

Personal response (relates to personal experience)

Recommendations for instruction

Portfolio Conference Questions on Reading

Name _____

Date _____

Reading Selection

Title _____

Type (circle as many as apply)

      fiction   nonfiction   poetry

      biography   content text   other:

What did you like best in the reading?

What strategies helped you read it?

What do you do to help you remember what you read?

What will you do to become a better reader?

Portfolio Conference Questions on Writing

Name_____

Date_____

Title of writing sample

_____

What do you like best about this piece of writing?

What strategies helped you write it?

How did you choose a topic for writing?

What will you do to become a better writer?

Portfolio Peer Assessment

Name _____

Your partner's name _____

Title of writing sample _____

1. Read your partner's writing sample.

2. What do you like best about your partner's writing?

3. What did your partner do well?

4. What do you think your partner could make better?

5. What advice would you give your partner?

Portfolio Self Assessment

Name _____ Date _____

Title of writing sample _____

1. Look at your writing sample.

2. What do you like best about your writing?

3. What did you do well?

4. How could you make your sample better?

5. What are your writing goals? Write one thing you need to do better.

About My Portfolio

1. What I Chose

2. Why I Chose It

3. What I Like and Don't Like

4. How My Work Has Changed

Introduction to the Graphic Organizers

1. Idea Web: This can be used for brainstorming activities in which students name the words they know about a topic. It can also be used to organize ideas into groups if circles with subtopics are added around the central circle.

2. K-W-L Chart: This can be used to introduce a theme, a lesson, or a reading. It can help generate students' interest in a topic and help students use their prior knowledge as they read. Students can complete the chart at the end of a unit or lesson.

3. T-Chart: This chart can be used to help students see relationships between information. It can be used to list cause (left column) and effect (right column) or to list words (right column) associated with a topic or story character (left column).

4. Venn Diagram: This can be used to help students understand comparisons and contrasts in a text. It can be used when the question asks, "How are the two things alike? How are they different?"

5. Story Sequence Chart: In this chart, students can list the beginning, middle, and end of a story and gain a sense of story structure.

6. Story Elements Chart: In this chart, students list the main elements of stories, including setting, characters, problems, and important events.

7. Main Idea Chart: This chart can be used to help students see and chart main ideas and supporting details.

8. Character Trait Web: In this chart, students can list the important qualities of characters in stories and how the characters' actions reveal those qualities.

9. Step Chart: This chart can be used to list events in sequence, such as events in a story or steps in a process.

10. Problem-Solution Chart: This chart is used to list problems and solutions in a story.

11. Word Log: Students can use this log to list important words in what they are reading or to list words that they want to learn.

Idea Web

K-W-L Chart

Topic: _____

What We **K**now	What We **W**ant to Know	What We **L**earned

T-Chart

Venn Diagram

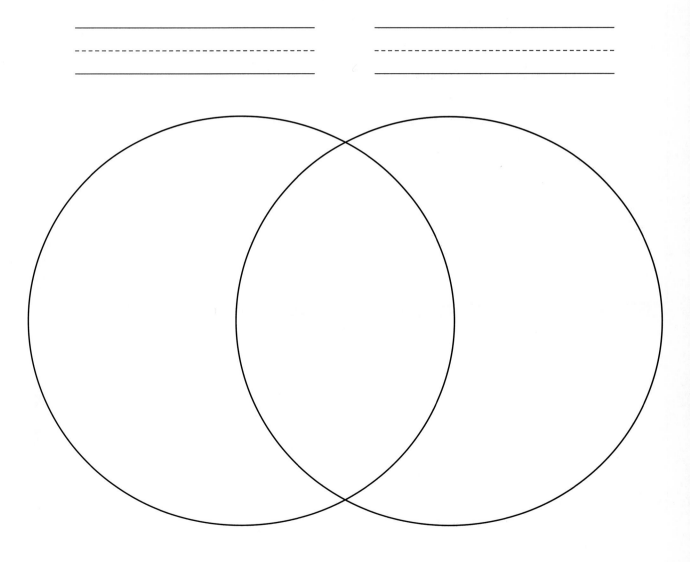

Story Sequence Chart

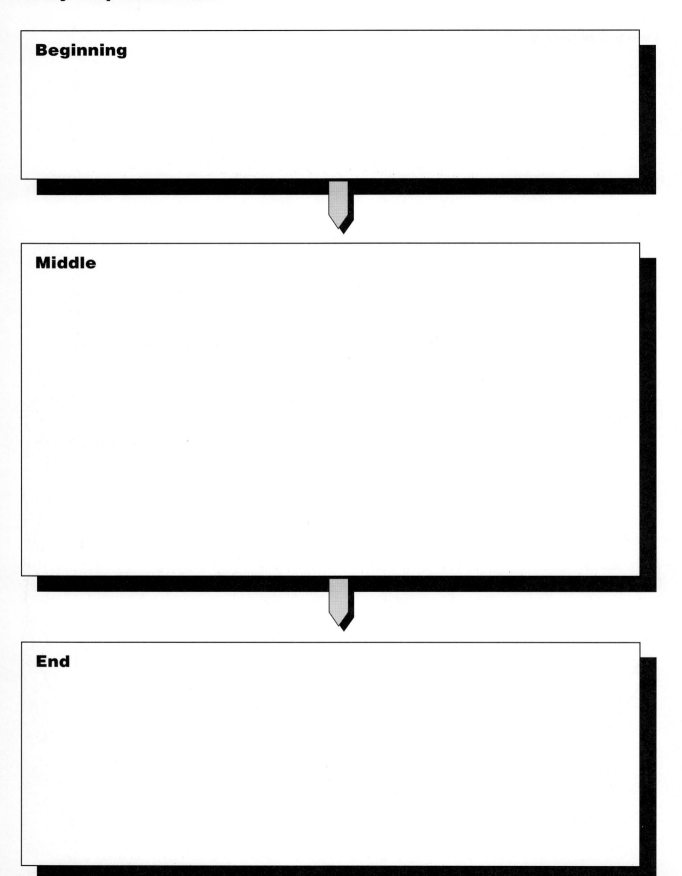

Beginning

Middle

End

Story Elements Chart

Title:

Setting:

Characters:

Problem:

Events:

Solution:

Main Idea Chart

Main Idea

Details

Character Trait Web

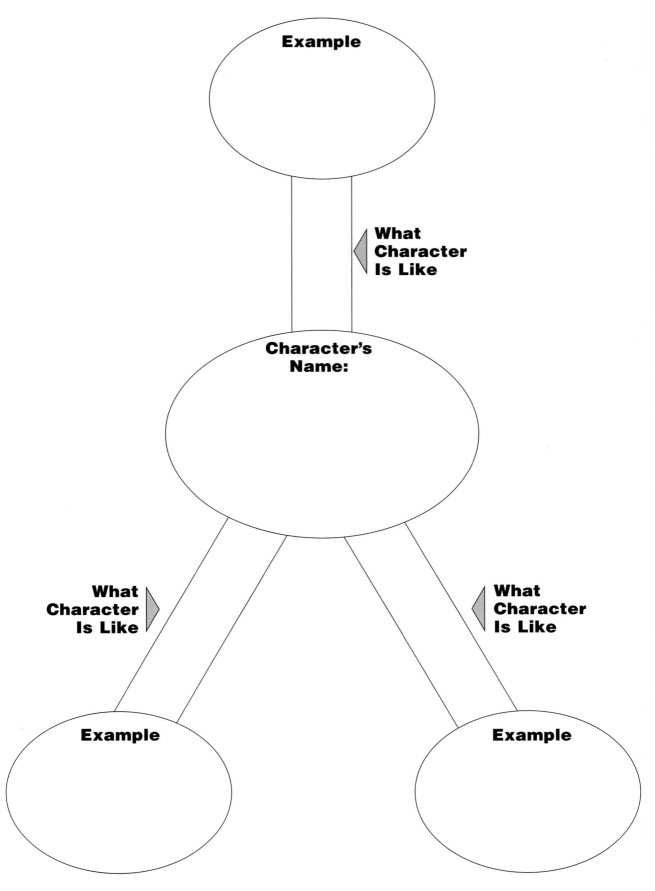

Step Chart

_____

- -

How to _____

1.

2.

3.

4.

5.

Problem-Solution Chart

Problem 1:

↓

Solution

Problem 2:

↓

Solution

Problem 3:

↓

Solution

Word Log

Date	New Words I Learned

Chapter Self Assessment

Name _____

Date _____

Chapter number _____

This chapter was about _____

Read each statement. Check (✔) the box that is most true for you.

Statement	Not very well	OK	Well	Very well
I understand the main ideas in the chapter.				
I can ask and answer questions about the main ideas.				
I can tell someone about the main ideas.				
I can write about the main ideas.				

Write something you learned in the chapter.

_____

_____

_____

_____

_____

_____

Dear Family,

Please come to

_____

_____

on_____

at _____ a.m./p.m. to see and hear about our latest project.
Taking a few minutes to visit with us can be an important part of
showing your child how important school is .

Please come.

Sincerely,

Teacher

Dear Family,

You are invited to see the latest class project your child has been working on. Please come to

_____

_____

on_____

at_____a.m./p.m.

You will be able to see what the class is learning and share in the learning process.

Thank you.

Sincerely,

Teacher

Dear Family,

For the next few weeks, our class will be studying how scientists learn about the past. Students will find out how scientists learn about dinosaurs (the study of paleontology) and how scientists learn about ancient cultures (the study of archaeology).

Students will make museum displays about dinosaurs and ancient Egypt. They will make models of various dinosaurs and prepare a display about ancient Egypt.

You may have things at home that the students can use to help prepare their displays. These things include

- markers
- cardboard

The class will use these things to prepare their museum displays.

Thank you for helping with our unit called "Digging Up the Past."

Sincerely,

Teacher

Apreciada familia:

Durante las próximas semanas, estudiaremos cómo investigan el pasado los científicos. Averiguaremos cómo recogen datos acerca de los dinosaurios (lo que se conoce como paleontología) y acerca de culturas antiguas (lo que se conoce como arqueología).

Los estudiantes prepararán exhibiciones de esculturas de dinosaurios y de escenas del antiguo Egipto. Harán varios modelos de dinosaurios y una exhibición del antiguo Egipto. Éstas son algunas de las cosas que se necesitan para este proyecto y que ustedes podrían aportar:

- marcadores
- cartones

Nos servirán para las exhibiciones. Gracias por colaborar al estudio de esta unidad titulada "*Digging Up the Past*" ("Desenterremos el pasado").

Atentamente,

Maestro/a

មកដល់គ្រួសាររបស់សិស្ស

ក្នុងរយៈពេលពីរបីសប្តាហ៍ខាងមុខនេះ កូនរបស់លោកអ្នកនឹងសិក្សាអំពីរបៀបដែលអ្នកវិទ្យាសាស្ត្រ ស្រាវជ្រាវរៀងអំពីអតីតកាល ។ គឺ សិស្សទាំងអស់នឹងស្វែងរកឲ្យដឹងនូវរបៀបដែលអ្នកវិទ្យាសាស្ត្រ ស្រាវជ្រាវអំពីសត្ថដំណាស់វ (ការសិក្សាបាសិណភូតវិទ្យា) និងរបៀប អ្នកវិទ្យាសាស្ត្រស្រាវជ្រាវរប្បធមិ៌ជំនាន់ដើម (បុរេវិទ្យា) ។

ដោយរាជាផ្នែកមួយនៃការសិក្សាវិជ្ជានេះ សិស្សានុសិស្សទាំងឡាយនឹងបង្កើតសារៈមន្ទីរមួយ ដែលមានតាំងរបស់សត្ថដំណាស់វ និងវត្ថុ បូរាណានៃសញ្ញាតិអេហ្ស៊ីប ។ លោកអ្នកប្រហែលជាមានវត្ថុដូចរៀបរាប់ខាងក្រោមនេះដើម្បីជួយដល់កូន ឲ្យយកមករៀបចំការជាក់ តាំងនៅសាលា ។ របស់ទាំងនេះមានដូចជា :

- បិចសំរាប់គូសចំណាំផំៗ
- ក្រដាសកាតុងសំរាប់គូរគំនូរ

សិស្សនឹងប្រើរបស់ទាំងនេះ ដើម្បីរៀបចំសារៈមន្ទីរនៅក្នុងសាលា ។ យើងសូមអរគុណលោកអ្នកដែលបានជួយដល់ការសិក្សារបស់ យើងដែលមានចំណងជើងថា "ការជីកស្រាវជ្រាវរៀងអតីតកាល" ។។

ហត្ថលេខា

គ្រូបង្រៀន

親愛的家長：

我們班上在下幾個星期中要學習科學家研究過去歷史的問題。學生要學習科學家怎樣研究恐龍(古生物學)及科學家怎樣研究古代文化(考古學)。

　同學們要作有關恐龍和古代埃及的博物館展覽。他們要作各種恐龍的模型，及準備古代埃及的展覽。

你家中可能會有他們準備這次展覽的東西。這些物件包括：

- 記號筆
- 紙板

班上同學要用這些東西準備他們的博物館展覽。謝謝你對我們「發掘過去」這一單元的幫忙。

忠誠地

老師

Chè Paran,

Nan semèn k ap vini yo, klas la pral etidye kouman syantis yo aprann sa ki te pase lontan. Elèv yo pral konnen kouman syantis yo etidye dinozò yo (etid sa a rele paleontoloji) epi kouman syantis yo etidye kilti ansyen tan yo (etid sa a rele Akeyoloji).

Elèv yo pral fè enstalasyon nan mize sou dinozò ansanm ak peyi Ejip nan tan lontan. Yo pral prepare yon vitrin sou divès dinozò ak youn sou Ejip.

Ou kab byen jwenn kichòy lakay ou elèv yo kab sèvi pou ede yo prepare enstalasyon sa yo. Men kèk bagay ou ka ba li:

- Majik makè yo
- Moso katon

Klas la pral sèvi ak bagay sa yo pou prepare enstalasyon yo.

Mèsi pou èd ou nan pati etid sa a ki rele "Fouye Fon nan Pase nou".

Avèk tout respè,

Pwofesè

Kính thưa quí vị phụ huynh

Trong vài tuần tới đây, các cháu sẽ học về cách thức các nhà khoa học nghiên cứu về quá khứ. Các cháu sẽ được biết cách thức các khoa học gia sưu tầm về các loại khủng long (khoa di tích học) và cách thức các khoa học gia sưu tầm về các nền văn hóa cổ (khoa khảo cổ học).

Các cháu sẽ thực hiện cuộc trưng bày di tích xưa về các con khủng long và về nước Ai Cập thời cổ. Các cháu sẽ lập nên các mô hình của vài loại khủng long và chuẩn bị cho cuộc trưng bày nước Ai Cập vào thời cổ. Có lẽ ở nhà quí vị có thể giúp cháu chuẩn bị cho các vật để trưng bày này. Chúng gao gồm:

• vài bút long màu
• thùng giấy

Các cháu sẽ dùng những món này để chuẩn bị cho buổi trưng bày di tích.

Xin cám ơn quí vị đã giúp cho bài học "Đào sâu Quá khứ" này.

Thành thật,

Giáo-viên

Name _____

Chapter 1 Language Assessment

A. Complete the sentences. Use the words in the box.

| era | meat-eaters | skeletons |
| fossils | plant-eaters | |

1. A large number of years is called an _____.

2. Scientists can tell which dinosaurs were _____ from their flat teeth.

3. Dinosaurs with sharp teeth were _____.

4. After millions of years, dinosaurs' teeth and bones turn into stone _____.

5. Scientists fit bones together to make _____.

B. Write **dinosaurs** after the facts about dinosaurs. Write **scientists** after the facts about scientists.

1. They divide history into eras and periods. _____

2. We know from their footprints that some of them were quick and nimble.

   _____

3. They get information by studying fossils. _____

4. Their name means "terrible lizards." _____

| dinosaur | egg | tooth | foot | fossil |

C. Fill in the blanks. Use words for more than one.

1. Some dinosaurs walked on four _____.

2. Meat-eaters have sharp _____.

3. Dinosaurs laid _____ just as birds do.

4. _____ lived before humans.

5. Dinosaur bones turned into _____.

Chapter 1 Listening Assessment

Listen carefully. Dr. Paleo has just found some fossils for a new dinosaur. Circle the pictures that show what Dr. Paleo has discovered.

1.

2.

3.

4.

5.

6.

Chapter 2 Language Assessment

A. Complete the sentences. Use the words in the box.

ancient	archaeologists	pyramids
mummies	hieroglyphics	pharaohs

1. The _____ Egyptians lived more than 3,000 years ago.

2. The _____ were Egyptian kings.

3. _____ are scientists who study about people who lived long, long ago.

4. Scientists discovered _____, which are preserved dead bodies wrapped in special cloth.

5. Tombs of some Egyptian kings were hidden in huge _____.

6. Scientists found _____ written on the walls of tombs.

B. Use the words in the box to label the artifacts.

furniture	game	jewelry	weapon

1. _____

2. _____

3. _____

4. _____

Chapter 2 Listening Assessment

Listen carefully. You will be told to draw items in the pyramid.
Draw the things you hear on the tape.

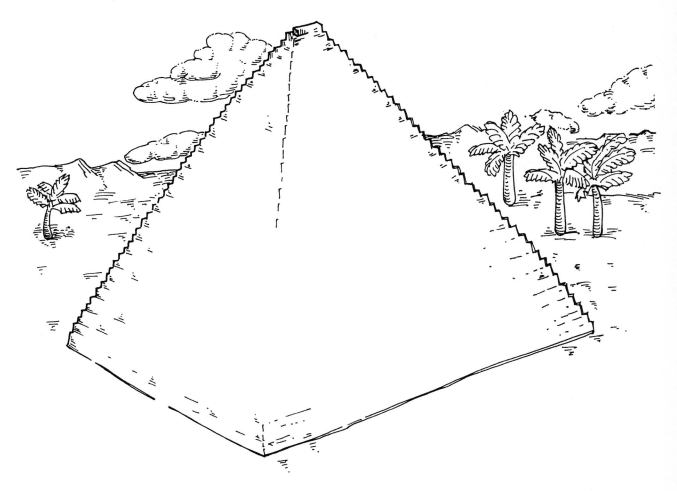

Dear Family,

For the next few weeks, our class will be studying games and sports. As part of the unit of study, we will have a class Olympics. Students will compete in different events.

Students will practice for their events at school and at home. You can help by reminding your child to practice.

You can also help by talking about games and sports in the country your family is from. Tell about these things:

- children's games
- popular sports for children and adults
- national sports teams
- famous athletes
- your country and the Olympics

Students will share this information with the class.

Thank you for helping with our unit about games and sports.

Sincerely,

Teacher

Apreciada familia:

Durante las próximas semanas, trataremos el tema de los juegos y los deportes. Como parte de esta unidad, realizaremos una olimpiada escolar con diversas competencias.

Los estudiantes entrenarán para las competencias tanto en la escuela como en la casa. Por favor, recuérdenle a su hijo/a que practique.

También podrían colaborar hablándole de los juegos y deportes propios de su país de origen, como por ejemplo:

- juegos infantiles
- deportes populares para niños y adultos
- equipos deportivos nacionales
- deportistas famosos
- participación del país en las olimpiadas

Los estudiantes transmitirán esta información al resto de la clase.

Gracias por ayudarnos con la unidad acerca de juegos y deportes.

Atentamente,

Maestro/a

មកដល់គ្រួសាររបស់សិស្ស

ក្នុងរយៈពេលពីរបីសប្តាហ៍ខាងមុខនេះ កូនរបស់លោកអ្នក និងសិក្សាអំពីល្បែងនិងកីឡា ។
ដោយរាជាផ្តៃកម្មយក្នុងការសិក្សាមេ រៀន នេះ យើងនិងមានបើកការប្រក្កតនៅក្នុងសាលារៀន
ហើយកូនសិស្សទាំងឡាយនិងធ្វើការប្រក្កតប្រជែងល្បែង និងកីឡាផ្សេងៗ ។ ដូច្នេះ
កូនរបស់លោកអ្នកនិងហាត់សំរាប់ការប្រក្កតនោះនៅផ្ទះ និងនៅសាលា ។
លោកអ្នកអាចជួយកូនរបស់ខ្លួនដោយជួយរៀ ពួកឲ្យកូនខំប្រឹងហាត់ ។

លើសពីនេះទៀត លោកអ្នកអាចជួយនិយាយប្រាប់កូនរបស់ខ្លួនអំពីល្បែង
និងកីឡាផ្សេងៗដែលមាននៅក្នុងស្រុកកំណើតរបស់ក្រុម គ្រួសារអ្នក ។ ចូរនិយាយប្រាប់កូននូវរឿងដូចតទៅនេះ៖

- ល្បែងកូនក្មេង
- កីឡាទាំងឡាយដែលក្មេងៗ និងមនុស្សចាស់ចូលចិត្ត
- ក្រុមកីឡាប្រចាំជាតិ
- ឈ្មោះកីឡាករល្បីៗ
- កីឡាអូឡាំពិចនិងប្រទេសរបស់លោកអ្នក

កូនសិស្សនិងយកពិតមាននេះ មកនិយាយប្រាប់មិត្តរួមថ្នាក់របស់គេ
ដូច្នេះយើងសូមអរគុណដល់លោកអ្នកដែលបានជួយក្នុងកម្មវត្ថុ សិក្សា អំពីល្បែង និងកីឡារបស់យើង ៕

ហត្ថលេខា

គ្រូបង្រៀន

親愛的家長：

在下幾個星期中，我們班上要學習有關遊戲和運動的問題。我們要舉辦一個班級奧運會。同學們將從事各項競賽。

同學們要在學校和家裡練習他們的項目。請提醒他們經常練習。

你也可以跟小孩談論你們家鄉的遊戲及運動。請跟孩子談論下列事項：

- 兒童遊戲
- 兒童及成人流行的運動
- 代表國家的運動代表隊
- 你國家和奧運的關係

同學們會把他們在家所學的帶到班上與其他同學分享。

謝謝你對我們「遊戲與運動」這一單元的幫忙。

忠誠地
老師

Chè Paran,

Nan semèn k ap vini yo, klas nou an pral etidye "Amizman" ansanm ak "Jwèt Espòtif". Pou yon pati nan etid la, klas la pral patisipe nan Jwèt Olenpik yo. Elèv yo pral nan konpetisyon nan diferan aktivite yo.

Elèv yo gen pou antrene pou aktivite yo ni lakay yo, ni lekòl la. Ou kab ede lè ou fè pitit ou sonje pou l antrene.

Ou menm paran kab ede ankò lè ou pale sou "Amizman ak Jwèt Espòtif" nan peyi kote fanmi an sòti. Pale de bagay sa yo:

- Jwèt timoun konn fè.
- Jwèt espòtif ki popilè pou timoun epi pou granmoun.
- Ekip espòtif nasyonal yo.
- Espòtmann ki gen gwo renome
- Peyi ou ak Olenpik yo

Elèv yo pral pataje enfòmasyon sa a ak klas la.

Mèsi pou èd ou ak pati etid nou sou "Amizman ak Jwèt Espòtif" yo.

Ak tou respè,

Pwofesè

Kính thưa quí vị phụ huynh

Trong vài tuần tới đây, các cháu sẽ học về các môn chơi thể thao. Trong phần của bài học này chúng tôi sẽ thực hiện một Thế Vận Hội cho lớp học. Các cháu sẽ tranh tài với nhau trong nhiều trận đấu khác nhau.

Để đấu trong các trận, các cháu sẽ phải tập dợt ở nhà và tập dợt ở trường. Quí vị có thể giúp cháu học bằng cách nhắc nhở cháu tập dợt.

Quí vị cũng có thể giúp bằng cách kể lại các môn thể thao ở quê hương xứ sở của quí vị. Hãy kể đến:

• các môn thể thao cho trẻ con
• các môn thể thao bình dân cho người lớn và cho trẻ con
• những đội banh quốc gia
• những cầu thủ nổi tiếng
• nước của quí vị và các nước trong Thế Vận Hội

Các cháu sẽ trao đổi chuyện này với lớp học.

Xin cám ơn quí vị đã giúp cho bài học các môn thể thao này.

Thành thật,

Giáo-viên

Chapter 3 Language Assessment

A. Label the parts of the body. Use the words in the box.

| elbow | heart | lung | muscle | shoulder |

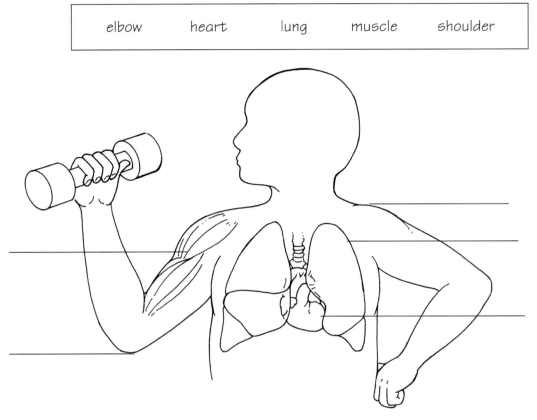

B. Draw lines from the kinds of fitness to their meanings.

Kinds of Fitness	**Meanings**
1. cardiovascular fitness	a. how easily you can move your joints
2. muscular endurance	b. how strong your heart and lungs are
3. flexibility	c. how much force your muscles can produce
4. strength	d. the amount of fat in your body
5. body fatness	e. how long you can use your muscles without getting tired

Chapter 3 Listening Assessment

Write the sentences you hear. They are steps in an exercise.

1. _____

_____

2. _____

_____

3. _____

_____

4. _____

_____

5. _____

_____

6. _____

_____

Chapter 4 Language Assessment

A. Complete the sentences with the past tense of the verbs in parentheses.

The Olympic games _____ (begin) in ancient Greece. Athletes _____ (go) to Olympia. There they _____ (compete) in such events as foot races and chariot races. The ancient games also _____ (include) speaking contests. The prize for winning _____ (is) a crown of leaves.

B. Complete the sentences. Use information from the chart. It shows the order runners finished in the race.

Runner	Time
Sonya	2 hours 45 minutes
Peter	2 hours 47 minutes
Carlos	2 hours 55 minutes
Miyoko	2 hours 56 minutes
Ana	2 hours 57 minutes

Example: Sonya finished ____first____ in the race.

1. Carlos finished _____ in the race.
2. Peter finished _____ in the race.
3. Ana finished _____ in the race.
4. Miyoko finished _____ in the race.

C. Write the sport next to its description.

baseball	diving	track and field	gymnastics

1. This is a team sport. _____
2. This sport is done in the water. _____
3. Races are part of this area of athletics. _____
4. This sport requires a high degree of balance and agility. _____

Chapter 4 Listening Assessment

Listen carefully. Circle the sports you hear talked about.

1.

2.

3.

4.

5.

6.

Dear Family,

For the next few weeks, our class will be studying oceans. We will build an ocean model in the classroom.

You can help your child learn about oceans. You may have things at home that students can use to build their models. These things include

- wax paper
- plastic wrap
- plastic shopping bags

Students will also learn about pollution. They will study ways to help protect the environment. You can help by talking about these topics:

- what things your family recycles
- how you prepare things to be recycled
- where you take things to be recycled
- what recycled products your family uses

Students will use these facts in class discussions of how to protect the environment.

Thank you for helping with our unit about oceans.

Sincerely,

Teacher

Apreciada familia:

Durante las próximas semanas, estudiaremos el tema de los mares y construiremos un modelo de un océano.

Para ayudar a su hijo/a en el aprendizaje de este tema, podrían aportar algunas cosas que necesitamos para este proyecto, como:

- papel encerado
- plástico de envolver
- bolsas grandes de plástico

También investigaremos acerca de la contaminación y de cómo proteger el medio ambiente. Les sugerimos que conversen con su hijo/a acerca de los siguientes temas:

- cosas que reciclan en su casa
- cómo las preparan para reciclarlas
- a dónde llevan los objetos de reciclaje
- qué productos reciclados usa la familia

Estos datos le servirán a su hijo/a para participar en las charlas acerca de la protección del medio ambiente.

Les agradecemos por ayudarnos con la unidad acerca de los mares.

Atentamente,

Maestro/a

មកដល់គ្រួសាររបស់សិស្ស

ក្នុងរយៈពេលពីរបីសប្ដាហ៍ខាងមុខនេះ ថ្នាក់រៀនរបស់យើង និងសិក្សាអំពីសមុទ្រ ។ ដូច្នេះ យើងនឹងបង្កើតសមុទ្រតូចមួយនៅក្នុង ថ្នាក់រៀន ។

លោកអ្នកអាចជួយបង្រៀនកូនខ្លួនអំពីសមុទ្រផងដែរ ដោយរកវត្ថុដូចតទៅនេះ៖ (ប្រសិនបើមាន) ដើម្បីឲ្យកូនយកមកសង់រូបសមុទ្រតូ នៅនឹងសាលា ។ របស់ទាំងនោះ មានដូចជា ៖

- ក្រដាសមានជាតិក្រមួន
- ផ្កាស្ទឹកសម្រាប់រាំ ឬខ្ចប់
- ថង់ផ្កាស្ទឹកដាក់ឥវ៉ាន់

សិស្សានុសិស្សនឹងសិក្សាអំពីភាពក្រខ្វក់របស់ទឹក និងរបស់បរិអាកាសផងដែរ ។ គេនឹងរៀនទូរវេប្បកការពារបរិយាកាស ដែលមាននៅជុំវិញខ្លួនយើងនេះ ។ លោកអ្នកអាចជួយ ដោយនិយាយប្រាប់កូនទូរវេរឿងទាំងឡាយដែលប្រធានដូចតទៅនេះ ៖

- របស់អ្វីដែលគ្រួសារលោកអ្នកតែងតែដាក់ក្នុងធុងសំរាម ដើម្បីឲ្យគេយកទៅវិលាយធ្វើជាអ្វីសំរាប់ប្រើឡើងវិញ
- របៀបដែលលោកអ្នករៀបចំរបស់ ទុកឲ្យគេយកទៅវិលាយធ្វើជាអ្វីមួយសំរាប់ប្រើសាជាថ្មី
- ទឹកទន្លេដែលលោកអ្នកដាក់របស់ ទុកឲ្យគេយកទៅវិលាយធ្វើជាអ្វីមួយសំរាប់ប្រើសាជាថ្មី
- ប្រដាប់ប្រដាដែលគេអាចយកទៅវិលាយធ្វើជាអ្វីមួយសំរាប់ប្រើសាជាថ្មីដែល ក្រុមគ្រួសាររបស់លោកអ្នក ទិញប្រើ ។

សិស្សានុសិស្សទាំងឡាយនឹងយករឿងនេះមកពិភាក្សាគ្នានៅក្នុងសាលា ហើយរកមធ្យោបាយការពារបរិយាកាសរបស់យើង ។ យើងសូមអរគុណលោកអ្នកដែលបានជួយដល់កម្មវិធីសិក្សាអំពីសមុទ្ររបស់យើង ៕

ហត្ថលេខា

គ្រូបង្រៀន

親愛的家長：

我們班上在下幾個星期中要學習海洋問題。我們要在班上建造一個海洋模型。

你可以在家幫孩子學習海洋。他們要學習保護環境的方法。跟孩子談論下列的題目會幫助他們了解這一單元的內容：

- 你家拿來循環使用的東西
- 你們怎樣準備要用來循環使用的東西
- 你們把東西拿到那裡去讓它們能重新被再次使用
- 你家用那些由循環使用材料製造的產品

同學們將用這些資料在班上討論保護環境的方法。

謝謝你們對我們「海洋」這一單元的幫忙。

忠誠地
老師

Chè Paran,

Nan semèn k ap vini yo, klas nou an pral etidye "Oseyan". Nou pral bati modèl yon oseyan nan klas la.

Ou kab ede pitit ou aprann kichòy sou etid oseyan yo. Siman ou genyen yon seri bagay lakay ou elèv yo kab sèvi pou bati modèl la. Sonje pou ba li pote:

- Papye wakse
- Papye plastik
- Sache plastik

Elèv yo pral aprann tou sou polisyon; yo pral etidye ki jan pou ede pwoteje anviwonnman an. Ou kab ede nou si ou pale sou sijè sa yo:

- Ki sa moun nan fanmi an resikle.
- Kouman ou prepare tout sa pou resikle yo.
- Ki kote pou ou pote tout sa ou genyen pou resiklaj.
- Ki pwodui resiklaj fanmi an sèvi.

Elèv yo pral sèvi ak tout enfòmasyon sa yo nan diskisyon yo sou jan pou pwoteje anviwonnman an.

Mèsi pou èd ou nan pati etid nou sou oseyan yo.

Ak tout respè,

Pwofesè

Kính thưa quí vị phụ huynh

Trong vài tuần tới đây, các cháu sẽ học về các biển cả. Chúng tôi sẽ tạo ra một mô hình biển cả trong lớp học.

Quí vị có thể giúp cháu học về biển cả. Có thể quí vị có vài món đồ mà các cháu sẽ dùng vào việc tạo ra mô hình biển cả. Những món đó bao gồm có:

- giấy sáp
- miếng ny lông mỏng
- bao ny lông

Các cháu sẽ học về sự ô nhiễm nữa. Các cháu sẽ nghiên cứu về những cách thức bảo vệ môi trường. Quí vị có thể giúp bàn về những đề tài sau đây:

- gia đình quí vị tái chu kỳ (dùng đi dùng lại) những món gì
- quí vị sắp xếp như thế nào trước khi cho món đồ đi vào tái chu kỳ
- quí vị mang các món đồ đến đâu để cho tái chu kỳ
- gia đình quí vị dùng những món đồ gì đã được tái chu kỳ

Các cháu sẽ sử dụng những sự kiện này để thảo luận trong lớp hầu để biết cách bảo vệ môi trường.

Xin cám ơn quí vị đã giúp đỡ trong bài học về biển cả này.

Thành thật,

Giáo-viên

Chapter 5 Language Assessment

A. Draw lines to match each ocean word with the sentence that tells about it.

Ocean Words

1. shore

2. salt water

3. sea animals

4. light zone

5. islands

6. trenches

7. coral reef

Sentences

a. This fills the ocean. You don't want to drink it!

b. Some of these are the tops of volcanoes.

c. These can be very, very deep.

d. These include fish, whales, and dolphins.

e. You will find shells here.

f. Many fish and plants live in this level of water.

g. These are found near the shore and have colorful fish.

B. Complete the sentences. Use the words in the box.

darker	less food	more light	warmer

1. Trenches are _____ than coral reefs.
2. Fewer fish live in the dark zone. There is _____ there.
3. Many plants live near the top of the ocean because there is _____ there.
4. The light zone is _____ than the dark zone.

Chapter 5 Listening Assessment

Listen carefully. Circle the areas of the ocean you hear talked about.
Circle the numbers you hear.

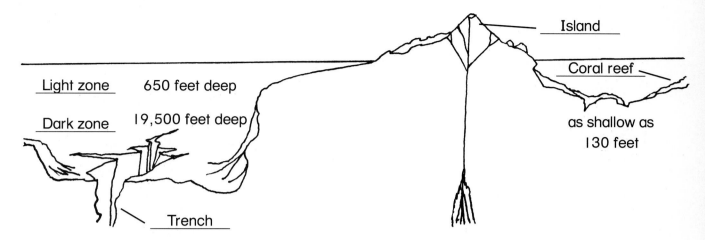

61

Chapter 6 Language Assessment

A. Complete the sentences. Use the words in the box.

agriculture	recycle
aquaculture	reduce
pollute	reuse

1. Fish farming is a form of _____.

2. Passing laws and using safe chemicals are ways to _____ pollution.

3. We can _____ plastic cups by washing them and using them again.

4. When we _____ newspapers, they can be used to make new paper.

5. People _____ the ocean with garbage and chemicals.

6. Growing animals and plants on land for food is called _____.

B. Write cause under the causes of pollution. Write effect under the effects of pollution.

1. Oil tankers spill oil into the oceans.

_____

2. People throw garbage on the beach and into the water.

_____

3. Animals are harmed and killed.

_____

4. Farmers use chemical fertilizers. These chemicals run into the ocean.

_____

5. Plants are harmed and killed.

_____

C. Complete the question with the correct word.

Who	What	Where	When	Why

_____ started the recycling project? Sixth-graders in Smith School.

_____ did they start the project? Last September.

_____ do they do? They collect cans of paper and take them to recycling centers.

_____ do they collect cans? They collect from areas around the school.

_____ did they start the project? They wanted to protect the environment.

Chapter 6 Listening Assessment

Listen carefully. Circle the projects that the school is doing.

1.
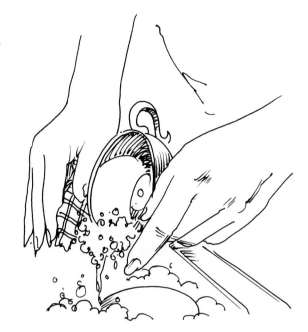

2.

3.

4.

Letter to the Family

Dear Family,

For the next few weeks, our class will be studying the ancient Romans. You can help your child learn more about the past.

Talk with your child about important events in the history of the country you are from. You might give information about these topics:

- the early history of your country
- main events in the history of the country

By providing this information, you will help your child better understand both the history of Rome and the history of your native country.

Students will be asked to make a simple costume to take part in a Roman Day. You can help gather some of the costume materials. These include

- old bed sheets
- string or cord

Thank you for helping us with our study of Rome and with our Roman Day.

Sincerely,

Teacher

Apreciada familia:

Durante las próximas semanas, estudiaremos el tema de los antiguos romanos.

Para ayudar a su hijo/a a entender el pasado, háblenle acerca de su país de origen. Pueden contemplar los siguientes temas:

- orígenes e historia patria
- principales sucesos históricos del país

Esta información le ayudará a su hijo/a a entender mejor tanto la historia de Roma como la de su país de procedencia.

Los estudiantes elaborarán un sencillo disfraz para participar en "El día de Roma". Quizá ustedes puedan aportar algunos de los siguientes materiales:

- sábanas viejas
- cuerdas o cordeles

Gracias por colaborar al estudio de los romanos y a la celebración del día dedicado a Roma.

Atentamente,

Maestro/a

Letter to the Family

មកដល់គ្រួសាររបស់សិស្ស

ក្នុងរយៈពេលពីរបីសប្ដាហ៍ខាងមុខនេះ ថ្នាក់រៀនរបស់យើងនឹងសិក្សាអំពីបុរាណកាលនៃជនជាតិរ៉ូមាំង ។ លោកអ្នកអាចជួយកូនលោក អ្នក ដោយបង្រៀនកូនអំពីរឿងអតីតកាល ។

ចូរនិយាយប្រាប់ក្មេងអំពីព្រឹត្តិការណ៍សំខាន់ៗ ដែលមាននៅក្នុងប្រវត្តិសាស្ត្រនៃមាតុភូមិរបស់លោកអ្នក ។ លោកអ្នកអាចនិយាយប្រាប់ នូវរឿងដែលមានប្រធានដូចតទៅនេះ

- ប្រវត្តិដំបូងនៃមាតុភូមិរបស់លោកអ្នក
- ព្រឹត្តិការណ៍ធំៗដែលមាននៅក្នុងប្រវត្តិសាស្ត្រនៃមាតុភូមិរបស់លោកអ្នក

ដោយការនិយាយប្រាប់នូវរឿងរ៉ាវដូចខាងលើនេះ លោកអ្នកនឹងជួយឲ្យក្មេង បានយល់កាន់តែច្បាស់អំពីប្រវត្តិសាស្ត្រទាំងពីរ គឺប្រវត្តិ សាស្ត្ររបស់ជនជាតិរ៉ូមាំង និងប្រវត្តិសាស្ត្រនៃមាតុភូមិរបស់លោកអ្នក។

យើងនឹងសុំឲ្យសិស្សទាំងអស់ធ្វើវត្ថុអ្វីមួយជាគំរូ ដែលបង្ហាញអំពីទំនៀមទម្លាប់ក្នុងសម័យដើមរបស់ជនជាតិរ៉ូមាំង ។ ដូច្នេះ លោកអ្នក អាចជួយរកសម្ភារៈដែលបង្ហាញពីទំនៀមទម្លាប់ឲ្យកូនរបស់លោកអ្នកបានស្គាល់ ។ របស់ទាំងនោះមានដូចជា :

- កំរាលព្រូកជំនាន់ដើម
- អំបោះ ឬខ្សែ

យើងសូមអរគុណដល់លោកអ្នក ដែលបានជួយដល់កម្មវិធីសិក្សា អំពីបុរាណកាលនៃជនជាតិរ៉ូមាំងរបស់យើង ៕

ហត្ថលេខា

គ្រូបង្រៀន

親愛的家長：

我們班上在下幾個星期中要學習有關古代羅馬的事蹟，你可以幫孩子多學習些有閱過去的事情。

跟你小孩談論你國家歷史上重要的事件。你可以談論下列的題目：
・你國家的早期歷史
・你國家歷史上的大事

跟孩子談論這些題目，可以令他們對羅馬歷史及你家鄉歷史有更深的了解。

我們要同學們準備一件簡單的服裝來參加學校的「羅馬日」。你可以幫孩子準備一些製造服裝的材料。這些材料可以是：
・舊床單
・細繩子或燈芯絨線 、

謝謝你對我們學習「羅馬」這一單元及我們「羅馬日」的幫忙。

忠誠地
老師

Chè Paran,

Nan semèn k ap vini yo, klas nou an pral etidye sou "Women" yo nan tan lontan. Ou kab ede pitit ou aprann plis sou tan lontan.

Pale ak pitit ou sou evennman enpòtan nan istwa peyi ou. Ou kab ba li enfòmasyon sou sijè sa yo:

- Istwa peyi ou depi nan kòmansman
- Evennman enpòtan nan istwa peyi w.

Lè ou bay pitit ou enfòmasyon sa yo, w ap ede pitit ou konprann pi byen istwa peyi Wòm ansanm ak istwa peyi w.

Nou pral mande elèv yo pou yo fè degizman senp pou yo sa fè pati jounen Women an. Ou kapab ede nou ranmase kèk materyèl pou fè degizman yo:

- Dra kabann (li pa bezwen nèf).
- Fisèl oswa kòd

Mèsi pou èd ou nan pati etid nou sou Wòm epitou ak jounen Women an.

Ak tout respè,

Pwofesè

Letter to the Family

Kính thưa quí vị phụ huynh

Trong vài tuần tới đây, cháu sẽ học về các người La Mã vào thời cổ. Quí vị có thể giúp cháu học thêm về quá khứ.

Quí vị cùng bàn với cháu về những sự kiện quan trọng trong lịch sử của quê hương xứ sở của quí vị. Thiết tưởng quí vị có thể cho biết các đề tài sau đây:

• lịch sử lúc ban đầu mới dựng nước
• những sự kiện chính xảy ra trong lịch sử sửa quê hương xứ sở quí vị

Khi cho biết các dữ kiện như vậy, quí vị giúp cháu hiểu rỏ cả vừa lịch sử của La Mã vừa lịch sử của chính quê hương xứ sở của quí vị.

Các cháu sẽ được yêu cầu làm ra một bộ y phục đơn giản để tham dự vào Ngày La Mã.

Quí vị có thể giúp cháu thâu nhặt vải để làm y phục này. Các món ấy gồm có :

• các miếng vải trải giường cũ
• dây thừng hoặc dây gai

Xin cám ơn quí vị đã giúp trong bài học La Mã và ngày La Mã.

Thành thật,

Giáo-viên

Chapter 7 Language Assessment

A. Complete the sentences. Use the words in the box.

aqueducts	arenas	forum	law	shops
arches	army	Latin	roads	temples

1. Roman _____ let rich men and poor men vote.
2. The Romans were the first to use _____ in their buildings.
3. The _____ was the center of the city and of government.
4. The Romans built _____ to honor their gods.
5. The Romans built _____ to connect Rome to other parts of the empire.
6. The Romans enjoyed sports events at _____.
7. People could get things they needed at _____ in the city.
8. The _____ language spread through the empire.
9. A strong Roman _____ helped the empire to grow.
10. The Romans built _____ to carry water to cities.

B. Complete the chart. Write the meaning of each prefix and the meaning of each word.

	Prefix	Words	Meaning of Prefix	Meaning of Word
1.	pre	pregame		
2.	re	rewrite		
3.	uni	unicycle		

C. Add the containers for the items used in the recipes. Use the words in the box. Use each phrase one time.

a bag of	a jar of	a bottle of	a carton of	a can of

_____ tuna

_____ honey

_____ dates

_____ eggs

_____ salad dressing

Chapter 7 Listening Assessment

Listen carefully. A student is talking about what she learned about the ancient Romans. Circle the places that she mentions.

1.

2.

3.

4.

5.

6.

Chapter 8 Language Assessment

A. The things listed in the box were found in the ashes of Pompeii. Some things were in houses. Some things were in other parts of the city. Write the five things that were in houses.

atrium	forum	shops
bakery	kitchen	snack bar
dining room	pots	temple
dishes	roads	

Things Found in Pompeii Houses

1. _____

2. _____

3. _____

4. _____

5. _____

B. Complete the sentences. Use the past tense of the words in the box.

come	run	sink
make	ring	watch

1. The farmer's plow _____ into the ground.
2. Smoke _____ out of the hole, and there were rumbling noises.
3. The farmer and his son _____ for the village.
4. The farmer _____ the bell to warn people.
5. All night, the people _____ the mountain grow.
6. The soldiers _____ people move away.

C. Write the words that relate to volcanoes on the lines. Then match each one to its definition.

erupt	flood	lava	storm	cinder	shield	hurricane

1. _____   a. burst out

2. _____   b. hot rock

3. _____   c. type of volcano

4. _____   d. pieces of burned rock

Chapter 8 Listening Assessment

Listen carefully. Write the sentences.

_____

_____

_____

_____

_____

_____

_____

_____

_____

Dear Family,

For the next few weeks, our class will be studying the physics of movement. Students will do experiments to learn basic science facts.

Your child will be participating in a project in which students describe and record examples of various types of motion that children engage in on playgrounds.

You can help your child learn. Ask him or her about the project on a regular basis.

You may have things at home that the class can use for its experiments and observations. These things include sport equipments such as

- soccer balls
- hockey sticks
- skates

Students will use these sports equipment to study friction, gravity, and other rules of physics.

Thank you for helping with our unit about physics.

Sincerely,

Teacher

Apreciada familia:

Durante las próximas semanas, estudiaremos la física del movimiento. Los estudiantes harán experimentos que les permitirán aprender conceptos científicos básicos.

Su hijo/a participará en un proyecto que consiste en describir y anotar ejemplos de los movimientos que hacen los niños en los patios de juego.

Para ayudar a su hijo/a en el aprendizaje del tema, pregúntenle con frecuencia cómo va el proyecto.

Para los experimentos y observaciones necesitamos algunos objetos que quizá ustedes puedan aportar:

- balones de fútbol soccer
- palos de hockey
- patines

Con ese equipo deportivo los estudiantes investigarán los conceptos de fricción, gravedad y otras reglas de la física.

Gracias por su colaboración en el estudio de esta unidad.

Atentamente,

Maestro/a

មកដល់គ្រួសាររបស់សិស្ស

ក្នុងរយៈពេលពីរបីសប្តាហ៍ខាងមុខនេះ ថ្នាក់រៀនរបស់យើង នឹងសិក្សាអំពីរូបវិទ្យានៃចលនា ។ សិស្សទាំងឡាយ និងធ្វើការពិសោធន៍ ដើម្បីរៀនភាពពិតដែលជាគោលនៃវិទ្យាសាស្ត្រ ។

កូនរបស់លោកអ្នក និងចូលរួមក្នុងសកម្មភាពមួយ ដែលសិស្សទាំងអស់នឹងកត់ទុកជាឯកសារ និងអធិប្បាយជាខទានារណ៍នូវសកម្មភាព ឆ្លើយឆ្លងរបស់ភ្នែកដែលកំពុងលេងនៅក្នុងស្ងួន ។ ដូច្នេះ លោកអ្នកអាចជួយកូនរបស់ខ្លួន ដោយសួរអំពីការងារវៃដែលគ្រដាក់ឲ្យនេះ ឲ្យ បានញឹកញាប់ និងទៀងទាត់ ។ នៅផ្ទះ លោកអ្នកប្រហែលជាមានរបស់ដូចរៀបរាប់ខាងក្រោមនេះ សំរាប់ឲ្យសិស្សប្រើក្នុងការធ្វើ កិច្ចពិសោធន៍ ស្រាវជ្រាវនេះហើយ ។ របស់ទាំងនោះមានដូចជា :

- បាល់ទាត់
- ឈើលេងហក់គី (Hockey)
- ស្បែកជើងដែលមានបាតធ្វើពីដែកស្រួចចាសំរាប់ពាក់ជើរលើទឹកកក

សិស្សនឹងយកសម្ភារៈកីឡាទាំងនេះទៅប្រើ ដើម្បីសិក្សាអំពីភាពត្រដុសឬកកិតគ្នា អំពីទំនាញផែនដី និងអំពីក្បួនដៃនៃរបស់រូបវិទ្យា ។ យើងសូមអរគុណដល់លោកអ្នក ដែលបានជួយដល់កម្មវិធីសិក្សារបស់យើង ៕

ហត្ថលេខា

គ្រូបង្រៀន

親愛的家長：

在下幾個星期中，我們班上要學習移動的物理作用。學生要做有關基本科學事實的實驗。

你的小孩要作一個研讀項目作業。在這個作業中學生們要描述和記錄小孩在操場上做的各種和動有關的活動。你可以在家幫他們學習這個題目，請經常查詢他們作業的進度。你家裡可能有班上能借用來作實驗和觀察的物件。這些物件多是運動器材，如：

- 足球
- 曲棍球球棍
- 溜冰鞋

同學們要用這些運動器材來學習磨擦力，地心引力，和其物理規則。

謝謝你對我們「物理作用」這一學習單元的幫忙。

忠誠地
老師

Chè Paran, ᵥb Zoo Txoa Tsev Neeg,

Nan semèn k ap vini yo, klas nou an pral etidye "Mouvman". Elèv yo pral fè eksperimantasyon pou yo aprann kèk fè a baz syantifik.

Pitit ou pral patisipe nan yon pwojè kote elèv yo pral dekri epi anrejistre anpil egzanp sou diferan tip mouvman timoun fè lè y ap jwe.

Ou kab ede pitit ou aprann. Mande l kesyon sou pwojè a regilyèman. Se sèten ou kab genyen kèk bagay lakay ou klas la kab sèvi pou fè eksperimantasyon ak obsèvasyon. Bagay sa yo enkli ekipman espò tankou:

- Boul foutbòl
- Bwa pou jwe hòki
- Paten

Elèv yo pral sèvi ak ekipman espò sa yo pou etidye friksyon, gravite ak lòt règleman syans fizik la.

Mèsi pou èd ou ak pati etid nou nan syans fizik la.

Ak tout respè,

Pwofesè

Kính thưa quí vị phụ huynh

Trong vài tuần tới đây, cháu sẽ học về các qui luật vật lý của động tác. Các cháu sẽ làm các thí nghiệm để học những sự việc khoa học căn bản.

Cháu sẽ tham gia vào một dự án trong đó các học sinh mô tả và ghi chép xuống những loại chuyển động mà trẻ con đang chơi trong sân trường.

Quí vị có thể giúp cháu học bằng cách thường xuyên hỏi về cái dự án ấy. Quí vị có thể có những món đồ ở nhà mà các cháu dùng được trong lớp để làm các bài thí nghiệm và quan sát. Những món đó bao gồm các dụng cụ thể thao như:

- trái banh
- que chơi hockey
- giầy trợt trên băng đá

Các cháu sẽ dùng những dụng cụ thể thao này để học về sự cọ sát, về trọng lượng, và về các qui luật vật lý khác.

Xin cám ơn quí vị đã giúp cho bài học vật lý này.

Thành thật,

Giáo-viên

Chapter 9 Language Assessment

A. Under each picture, write the word that tells about the action. Use the words in the box.

blow	kick	pull
jump	push	throw

1. _____

2. _____

3. _____

4. _____

5. _____

6. _____

B. Draw a line from each word to its definition.

Words

1. motion

2. force

3. friction

4. gravity

Meanings

a. the force that draws objects toward the center of the earth

b. the force that slows down the motion of surfaces that touch

c. the movement of an object from one place to another

d. the power to cause motion, or to stop or change motion

Chapter 9 Listening Assessment

Listen carefully. For each item, circle the pictures you are told to circle.

1.

2.

3.

Chapter 9 Language Assessment

A. Complete the sentences. Use the words in the box.

curves	motor	down
stops	motion	work

1. Energy is the ability to do _____.
2. A roller coaster builds up energy from _____.
3. A roller coaster needs a _____ to climb the first hill because it hasn't built up any energy yet.
4. A roller coaster uses energy from going _____ the first hill to go up the second hill.
5. When a roller coaster goes on twists and _____, it uses energy.
6. When a roller coaster uses up all its energy, it _____.

B. The words in the box all tell ways to move. Write each word under the heading that tells whether it means to move slowly or to move quickly.

crawl	inch	rush	zoom
dash	lumber	stroll	

To move slowly

_____

_____

_____

_____

To move quickly

_____

_____

_____

_____

C. Complete the conditional sentences. Use the verb in parentheses.

1. If I rode a roller coaster for two days, I _____ (be) tired.
2. If I could ride any roller coaster, I _____ (want) to ride the Cyclone.
3. If I could build a roller coaster, it _____ (have) a lot of curves.
4. If I could go on a tall roller coaster, I _____ (be) very excited.

Chapter 10 Listening Assessment

Listen carefully. Follow the directions. Number the pictures of the roller coaster.

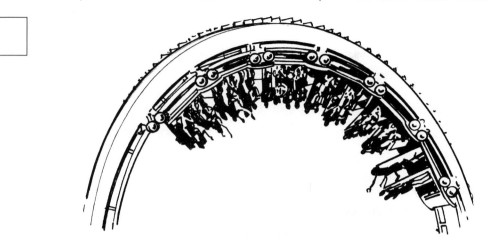

Letter to the Family

Dear Family,

For the next few weeks, our class will be studying various aspects of change, including handling stress.

As part of the unit, students will act out skits about situations that can cause stress, such as moving to a new place or starting in a new school. They will also prepare a class magazine that focuses on changes in life situations.

You can help your child better understand what the class is studying by discussing these topics:

- changes that your family has faced since you moved to the United States
- ways your family handles changes as they come along

Thank you for helping us make the project a successful one.

Sincerely,

Teacher

Apreciada familia:

Durante las próximas semanas, estudiaremos varios aspectos del cambio. Uno de ellos es cómo manejar la tensión nerviosa.

Como parte de la unidad, los estudiantes representarán escenas teatrales sobre situaciones que pueden causar estrés, tales como el traslado a un nuevo lugar o el ingreso a una nueva escuela. Además, harán una revista colectiva dedicada a diversos cambios en la vida.

Para ayudar a su hijo/a a entender mejor el tema, conversen acerca de lo siguiente:

- Cómo ha cambiado su vida desde que llegaron a los Estados Unidos.
- Cómo ha enfrentado la familia esos cambios.

Gracias por ayudarnos con la realización de este proyecto.

Atentamente,

Maestro/a

មកដល់គ្រួសាររបស់សិស្ស

ក្នុងរយៈពេលពីរបីសប្ដាហ៍ខាងមុខនេះ ថ្នាក់រៀនរបស់យើង នឹងសិក្សាអំពីទស្សនៈទាំងឡាយនៃការផ្លាស់ប្ដូរ ហើយនិងវិធីដោះ ស្រាយវិបត្តិ ។

ដោយវាជាផ្នែកមួយនៃការសិក្សា កូនសិស្សជាច្រើននឹងសម្ដែងជារឿងមួយ ដោយស្ដីអំពីស្ថានការណ៍ដែលបណ្ដាលឲ្យកើតមានវិបត្តិ ដូចជា ការផ្លាស់ទៅនៅក្នុងកន្លែងថ្មីមួយ ឬការចូលទៅរៀននៅក្នុងសាលាថ្មីមួយជាដើម ។ លើសពីនេះ សិស្សទាំងឡាយនឹងរៀប ជាទស្សនាវដ្ដីសំរាប់សិក្សាមួយ ដែលនិយាយអំពីការផ្លាស់ប្ដូ រស្ថានភាពក្នុងការរស់នៅ ។

លោកអ្នកអាចជួយក្នុងឲ្យយល់បន្ថែមទូរអ្វីដែលយើងកំពុងសិក្សានេះ ដោយពិភាក្សាទូររឿងទាំងឡាយដែលមានប្រធានដូចតទៅនេះ៖

- ការផ្លាស់ប្ដូរដែលក្រុមគ្រួសាររបស់លោកអ្នកបានជួបប្រទះ៖ នៅពេលដែលបានធើ្វមកនៅក្នុងសហរដ្ឋអាមេរិកនេះ
- របៀបដែលក្រុមគ្រួសាររបស់លោកអ្នក ដោះស្រាយបញ្ហាពីការផ្លាស់ប្ដូរនេះ៖ នៅពេលដែលខ្លុំ្ញនបានជួបប្រទះ៖

យើងសូមអរគុណលោកអ្នក ដែលបានជួយធ្វើឲ្យកម្មវិធីសិក្សារបស់យើងនេះ បានសម្រេច ៕

ហត្ថលេខា

គ្រូបង្រៀន

親愛的家長：

我們班上在下幾個星期中要學習有關變遷的各種情況，包括對生活壓力的處理方法。

班上同學將演出各種能製造生活壓力情況的短劇，例如搬到新地區或到新學校上課的情況等。他們還要編寫一份和生活改變有關的雜誌。

如果你能和孩子討論下列的題目，這能幫助他們對班上所學的有更深的認識：

- 你們搬來美國所遭遇的變遷
- 你們家裡處理生活壓力的方法

謝謝你幫我們使這一研讀項目成功。

忠誠地
老師

Chè Paran,

Nan semèn k ap vini yo, klas nou an pral etidye diferan aspè sou "Chanjman ansanm ak kouman pou nou sòti anba Estrès".

Nan pati etid nou an, elèv yo pral jwe yon pyès teyat sou sitiyasyon ki pral bay estrès, oswa tet chaje, tankou brote al yon lòt kote oswa kòmanse nan yon nouvo lekòl. Yo pral prepare yon revi ki pral fikse sou chanjman ki genyen nan sitiyasyon lavi a.

Ou kab ede pitit ou konprann pi byen sa klas la ap etidye si ou pale avèk li sou sije sa yo:

• Chanjman fanmi w te fè fas a yo lè yo rantre Ozetazini,
• Fason fanmi an degaje yo ak tout chanjman k ap vini sou yo.

Mèsi pou èd ou ak pwojè a ki ap gen siksè.

Ak tout respè,

Pwofesè

Kính thưa quí vị phụ huynh

Trong vài tuần tới đây, các cháu sẽ học về nhiều trạng thái của sự thay đổi, kể cả cách xử sự trước tình trạng căng thẳng tinh thần.

Trong phần của bài học này các cháu sẽ giả đóng tuồng về các hoàn cảnh có thể gây ra sự căng thẳng tinh thần, như dọn nhà đi nơi khác và khởi đầu đi học trường mới. Các cháu cũng soạn thảo ra một cuốn báo ảnh cho lớp, đặt trọng tâm vào những sự thay đổi trong các hoàn cảnh của cuộc đời.

Quí vị có thể giúp cháu hiểu rõ hơn về các bài học ở trong lớp bằng cách thảo luận những đề tài sau đây:

- những sự thay đổi mà gia đình phải chịu từ khi dọn đến ở Hoa Kỳ
- các phương cách mà gia đình dùng để xoay sở khi gặp tình trạng thay đổi

Xin cám ơn quí vị đã giúp đỡ chúng tôi hoàn thành dự án này được mỹ mãn.

Thành thật,

Giáo-viên

Chapter 11 Language Assessment

A. Write each word from the box under the picture where it belongs.

angry	happy	sad	worried
excited	nervous	scared	

Pleasant Feelings   **Unpleasant Feelings**

_____   _____

_____   _____

_____   _____

_____   _____

_____   _____

B. Draw lines from the words to their definitions.

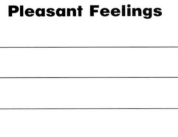

Words	**Definitions**
1. stress	a. the act of sweating
2. emotion	b. quick in thought or action
3. alert	c. any strong feeling
4. perspiration	d. a hormone that speeds up the heartbeat
5. adrenaline	e. strain or pressure

Chapter 11 Listening Assessment

Listen carefully. Draw lines
from the words to the pictures
you hear described.

1. Student 1

2. Student 2

Chapter 12 Language Assessment

A. Complete the sentences. Use the words in the box.

computer	encyclopedia	magazine	newspaper	textbook

1. A _____ is what you bring to class almost every day.
2. An _____ is a set of books that has information about almost any subject.
3. A _____ is often published every day. You use it to find out what is happening in the world or in your community.
4. A _____ is an electronic device that stores information.
5. A _____ is a publication that usually comes out every week or every month. It contains articles and pictures.

B. Read the article. Then answer the five W questions below.

On Saturday, October 15, sixth-graders from Fulton Middle School will collect plastic and newspaper to recycle. They want to help the environment. Students will collect one box of newspaper and two bags of plastic from around their neighborhoods.

1. Who? _____

2. What? _____

3. When? _____

4. Where? _____

5. Why? _____

Chapter 12 Listening Assessment

Listen carefully. Write the words.

_____   _____

_____   _____

_____   _____

_____   _____

_____   _____

_____   _____

Answers

Language Assessment

page 40:
A. 1. era
2. plant-eaters
3. meat-eaters
4. fossils
5. skeletons
B. 1. scientists
2. dinosaurs
3. scientists
4. dinosaurs
C. 1. feet
2. teeth
3. eggs
4. Dinosaurs
5. fossils

page 42:
A. 1. ancient
2. pharaohs
3. archaeologists
4. mummies
5. pyramids
6. hieroglyphics
B. 1. game
2. weapon
3. jewelry
4. furniture

page 50:
A. Check that the labels point to the appropriate body parts.
B. 1. b
2. e
3. a
4. c
5. d

page 52:
A. began, went, competed, included, was
B. 1. third
2. second
3. fifth
4. fourth
C. 1. baseball
2. diving
3. track and field
4. gymnastics

page 60:
A. 1. e
2. a
3. d
4. f
5. b
6. c
7. g
B. 1. darker
2. less food
3. more light
4. warmer

page 62:
A. 1. aquaculture
2. reduce
3. reuse
4. recycle
5. pollute
6. agriculture
B. 1. cause
2. cause
3. effect
4. cause
5. effect
C. Who, When, What, Where, Why

page 70:
A. 1. law
2. arches
3. forum
4. temples
5. roads
6. arenas
7. shops
8. Latin
9. army
10. aqueducts
B. 1. before, before the game
2. again, write again
3. one, a cycle with one wheel
C. a can of, a jar of, a bag of, a carton of, a bottle of

page 72:
A. 1. atrium
2. dishes
3. pots
4. dining room
5. kitchen
B. 1. sank
2. came
3. ran
4. rang
5. watched
6. made
C. 1. erupt, a
2. lava, b
3. cinder, d
4. shield, c

page 80:
A. 1. pull
2. kick
3. push
4. jump
5. blow
6. throw
B. 1. c
2. d
3. b
4. a

page 82:
A. 1. work
2. motion
3. motor
4. down
5. curves
6. stops
B. To move slowly: crawl, inch, lumber, stroll; To move quickly: rush, zoom, dash
C. 1. would be
2. would want
3. would have
4. would be

page 90:
A. Pleasant Feelings: happy, excited; Unpleasant Feelings: angry, sad, worried, nervous, scared
B. 1. e
2. c
3. b
4. a
5. d

page 92:
A. 1. textbook
2. encyclopedia
3. newspaper
4. computer
5. magazine
B. 1. sixth-graders from Fulton Middle School
2. The students will collect plastic and newspaper to recycle.
3. On Saturday, October 15
4. In their neighborhoods
5. Because they want to help the environment

Listening Assessment

page 41: Numbers 3 and 5 should be circled.

page 43: There should be a mummy drawn in the pyramid, as well as one artifact such as a chair or jewelry.

page 51: The sentences should match the tapescript. See page T40c in the Teacher's Edition.

page 53: Numbers 1, 3, and 6 should be circled.

page 61: Coral reef, dark zone and *19,500 feet deep.*

page 63: Numbers 1 and 3 should be circled.

page 71: Numbers 1 and 5 should be circled.

page 73: The sentences should match the tapescript. See page T116d in the Teacher's Edition.

page 81: The following should be circled: 1. the girl throwing the ball 2. the ball rolling across the grass 3. the store clerk dropping a can

page 83: The roller coaster in a loop should be numbered 2 and circled; the roller coaster car stopping should be numbered 3 and there should be a line through the picture; the roller coaster going up the hill should be numbered 1 and should be Xed.

page 91: 1. girl in a messy room 2. boy shooting a basketball

page 93: Here are the words in alphabetical order: article, facts, information, newspaper, people, places, things